# It must be a Senior Moment

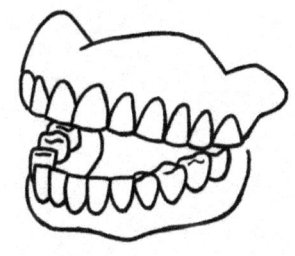

~

In no way inspired by *wink wink* but 100% dedicated to:

Granny and Gramps Page

&

Grandma and Grandad Parker

~

# By Gemma Denham

www.gemmadenham.com

Published by Elizabeth Publications
Available from Amazon.com and other retail outlets
Available on Kindle and other devices

Text and illustration copyright © Gemma Denham 2020
Moral rights asserted.

All rights reserved. No part of this publication may be reproduced,
stored in a retrieval system, or transmitted, in any form or by any means
without prior permission of the author.

ISBN 978-1-9163584-0-9

# Contents

| | | |
|---|---|---|
| Making a Spectacle | | 14 |
| Socks and Sandals | | 16 |
| Why? | | 18 |
| Bald Eagle | | 20 |
| Whatsername | | 22 |
| Riding High | | 24 |
| Sprouting | | 26 |
| Story Lines | | 28 |
| The Good, the Bad and the Oldie | | 30 |
| Afternoon Nap | | 32 |
| Swing Low | | 34 |
| Going Nowhere Slow | | 36 |
| Eh? | | 38 |
| The Art of Movement | | 40 |
| Night | | 42 |
| Remember | | 44 |
| Early Bird Special | | 46 |
| Beige | | 48 |
| Slow Lane | | 50 |
| Retirement | | 52 |
| Queue | | 54 |
| Manhood | | 56 |
| The Doctor Will See You Now | | 58 |

| | | |
|---|---|---|
| EARLY | | 60 |
| I AM NOT OLD | | 62 |
| PILL POPPIN' | | 64 |
| FORGETTER | | 66 |
| FATHER'S CHAIR | | 68 |
| MOT | | 70 |
| COMPUTER SAYS NO | | 72 |
| OLDER THAN I SHOULD BE | | 74 |
| 50 SHADES OF BEIGE | | 76 |
| MY WAY | | 78 |
| OF AGE | | 80 |
| AGE TEST | | 82 |
| LOST | | 84 |
| I AM OLD | | 86 |
| GRUMBLES | | 88 |
| PIPE AND SLIPPERS | | 90 |
| I AM GRANDAD | | 92 |
| GOOD FOR WHAT AILS YOU | | 94 |
| OLD FART | | 96 |
| I AM GRANNY | | 98 |
| BACK IN MY DAY | | 100 |
| BUS PASS | | 102 |
| CHANGE | | 104 |
| LOOKS GOOD TO ME | | 106 |
| VOLUME CONTROL | | 108 |
| CHARM & GRACE | | 110 |
| HOW OLD? | | 112 |
| I'D RATHER DYE | | 114 |

| | | |
|---|---|---|
| Key to Success | | 116 |
| To Pee or Not to Pee | | 118 |
| Dinner Time | | 120 |
| My Hands | | 122 |
| Revenge | | 124 |
| Life Happens When You're Busy | | 126 |
| Poor Old Pensioners | | 128 |
| Always Read The Label | | 130 |
| Doolally | | 132 |
| With Thanks | | 134 |

## Making a Spectacle

"Where have I put my glasses down?"
Grandpa said, wearing a frown.
"Those things have disappeared from sight"
"And I have searched with all my might."
There came a booming laugh from Millie.
"Ha ha ha! You are so silly!"
"Oh my dear old Grand-pa-pa"
"They really haven't gone that far"
"You'll surely give yourself a flogging"
"Cause they lay upon your noggin!"
And sure enough, that they did.
The little buggers hadn't hid.
They hadn't upped away and fled.
Just sat atop of Grandpa's head!

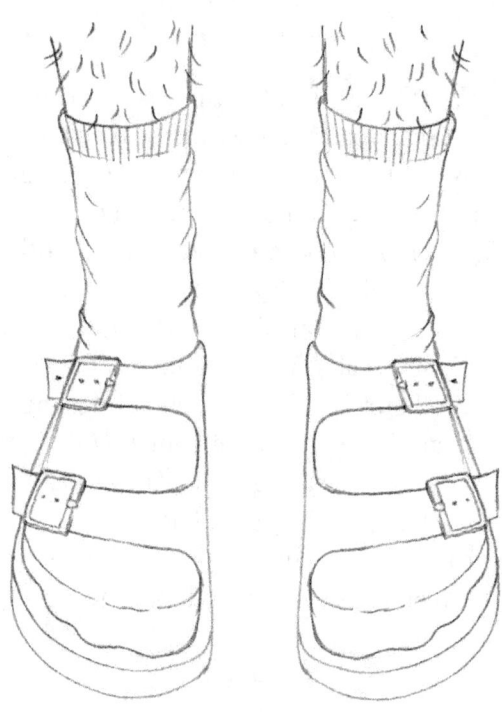

## Socks and Sandals

At what age do we just not care
About the things we choose to wear?
The feet must be the first to go
I'll tell you why, so that you know.
The biggest one to cause most shocks
Is wearing sandals with your socks!
Please do not let me get that bad.
I will not dress like my Grandad.
The fashion faux pas' final straw
It should be made against the law.
A sandal worn alone is fine,
A sandal can be quite divine.
To add a sock – you kill it dead
Something's amiss inside your head.
The two items should never meet
And least of all upon your feet.

# WHY?

I've come on a little wander
Something I have to get
Something that is important
But what, I do forget
It will come back in a minute
I'm sure it will reappear
Damn, blast and bugger it!
Why did I come in here?

I'll go back to where I started
To jog the memory free
Create an action replay
Then it'll come to me
I feel I've nearly got it
It's there but still unclear
Damn, blast and bugger it!
Why did I come in here?

Oh this is frustrating
I can't admit defeat
Ten minutes I have stood here now
And still it has me beat!
It's no use I have lost it
It's gone for good I fear
Damn, blast and bugger it!
Why did I come in here?

# Bald Eagle

Upon my head there used to be,
The most luscious locks you'd care to see.
My head was full, my hair was thick,
And at the front I'd wax a flick.
But slowly as the years marched on,
I noticed something going wrong.
My crown began to show some skin,
My luscious locks were growing thin!
Oh no. Not me. This isn't fair.
Please do not take away my hair.
The patch kept going getting thinner,
Doubled in size it seemed by dinner.
And the rest it's fair to say,
Was black no more, but going grey!
What fate has fell upon my head?
I'd rather grey then see them fled!
Oh dearie me, I do despair.
Please won't you help me find my hair.

# Whatsername

I'm a source of much amusement.
My family take the mickey.
Because I will forget the name
And call it the doohickey.
The whatchamacallit, the thingamajig,
The doodah or the whatsit.
Embarrassing and frustrating,
Yes I know I am a nitwit.
And should I have to call someone
By their actual name?
Well, what a palaver,
That is a sodding game!
I'll list every God damn name
There is under the sun.
We could be here for hours
Before I find the right one.
No person, place or object
Can be saved from my brain.
The information's in there
It's just hard to find again!

# Riding High

I've come to realise that with age,
Some body parts can get mislaid.
I'll give an example with my waist,
For years that buggers been misplaced.
It used to sit above my hips,
But now it's closer to my nips.
My trousers – well I wear them high
At least it keeps the bottoms dry
- No wet ankles anymore,
They hang quite safely off the floor.
My belly is tucked all snug inside,
My rolls and wobbles can all hide.
No longer do I feel restricted,
The results are not unpredicted.
Such comfort, well I can't deny,
Is found when wearing trousers high.

## Sprouting

You may think that my hair is gone,
But I can prove that it still grows.
You'll find it thick and plentiful,
If you look inside my nose.
You see I once got startled,
And in fright it left my head.
Looking for a hiding place,
It chose my nose instead.
Although it wouldn't all quite fit
But wanting to stay near,
The rest went around the sides,
and found home inside an ear.

## Story Lines

So many wrinkles on my face
And lines for all to see.
Each one a laugh or worry,
Each one its own story.
They show you that I've lived my life,
They show you that I've cared.
Around my eyes show that I've laughed,
Forehead – that temper's flared.
The lines of my life story,
I wear with pride and grace.
I just wish they were inside a book
And not written upon my face!

# The Good, the Bad and the Oldie

Can anybody tell me please
Just what has happened to my knees?
They once were known as left and right
Before that one gave up the fight.
It's now appropriate you should
Refer to them as bad and good.

I cannot sit upon the floor
If in time I wish to stand once more.
I'd need a hoist, I'd need a cane,
Or friendly neighbour with a crane.
I fear it is the only way
Else once I'm down I'm here all day.

I have now taken to the car
As my poor knee can't walk that far
Unless the path is level – fine
But should there be a slight incline?
Well that would be the end I'm sure
The likes of me would be no more!

## Afternoon Nap

Dear Grandma sat upon her chair
All comfortable and snug in there
And like the norm was fast asleep
She didn't stir or make a peep
Until a rumble and a roar
As she let out a mighty snore
So loud for someone of her size
She came to and opened up her eyes
She seemed confused, she seemed quite dazed
But even in her sleep filled haze
Said "I was just resting my eyes!"
(Which came as no real great surprise)
"I do not nap, that much is true"
"that's something that old people do"
"and I am nowhere near that stage"
"I'm very spritely for my age."
We chuckled but we let it go
Deep down we thought that she must know
And so we carried on till when
We noticed Grandma nod again.

# Swing Low

How my boobs swing low
Watch them wobble to and fro
I could tuck them in my pants
If it weren't for my implants
They would knock me to the ground
If I were to run around
How my boobs
Swing
Low.

How my boobs do flap
I can even make them clap
If it wasn't for my bra
Well I wouldn't get that far
They rub enough to start a fire
But that is of no desire
How my boobs
Do
Flap.

## Going Nowhere Slow

With a creak and a groan
I rise from my seat.
My legs are unstable,
There's pain in my feet.
I'm up but although
My mind maybe ready,
These things take time
And my body's unsteady.
I flex and I arch,
To stretch out my back.
I don't stop the process
Until it goes crack.
A swing and a rotate
To loosen the hip.
The left one is fine
But the right gives me jip.
Nearly complete now
Just the knees remain.
A few bends and stretches
Prevents any pain.
I'm ready to go
But I stand with a frown.
I forgot why I'm up
So I'd better sit down.

# EH?

Our conversations, one might say
Have a tendency to go astray.
The problem that is fast appearing
Is we *may be* getting hard of hearing.
I do say we, but mostly him.
It's that or he is not tuned in,
And focused on some other task
So he won't even hear me ask.
Or he'll answer what he's thought he's heard
And well, that turns things quite absurd,
When I'm half way into my flow,
It's suddenly clear he does not know,
As he talks completely unabated,
Of something totally unrelated.
I get quite cross; he's unaware,
I'm slowly tearing out my hair.
The both of us go round, and round,
Until we find the common ground.
A two minute story – half an hour long.
Please someone put the kettle on.

## The Art of Movement

I know I am not on my own,
With every movement causing a groan.
It's not a conscious choice you see,
But something that's happened to me.
I know not if it has a gain,
I'm not in any kind of pain.
It's just something that must be done,
To give me enough momentum.
I shout when rising out my chair,
I grumble walking here to there,
An 'ooh-yer!' gets me off the floor,
(Though I'm rarely down there anymore)
Even turning in my bed,
Will lead to something being said.
Some find it strange, it can confuse,
To others? Well it does amuse.

# Night

No longer I'm the night owl,
And with this news I'm fine.
Always in bed by 10 O'clock ,
Sometimes nodded off by 9.

I schedule my viewing round this.
Won't start a film too late.
It truly is preposterous,
To consider anything after 8.

A meal out in the evening?
Let's make it lunch instead.
Otherwise it'll be cut short,
To get back home to bed.

It's not as if we've planned this.
We'd stay up later if we could.
But once bedtime has struck,
We're snoring in all likelihood.

# Remember

There are two things to remember,
Two things I must not forget.
There is one thing I must post,
And one thing that I need to get.
I'll keep the letter in my hand,
A reminder to me.
The other thing – a pint of milk,
So I can make some tea.
I'm suited and I'm booted,
So I leave and lock the door.
There are two things to remember,
Only two and nothing more.
The walk down to the high street,
Is quite nice, it isn't long.
Some friendly faces say hello,
The air full of bird song.
I get there, take a basket,
And I think back in my head.
Two things to remember,
So I grab some milk and bread.

My mission is complete,
And so I pay and leave the door.
Two things remembered and now got,
Two things and nothing more.
Back home I flip the kettle on,
But then I stop and stand.
I'm halfway out my coat,
But there's a letter in my hand.
I'm unsure how it got there,
I just stare at it blankly.
The confusion slowly lifting,
As it all comes back to me.
Well, what a wally that I feel,
I tut and roll my eyes.
I'd like to say it's the first time,
But it is no great surprise.
I'll leave it by the front door,
In plain sight so that way then,
When I leave the house tomorrow,
I can go and try again.

## Early Bird Special

I really do not wish to grumble,
But in my belly there's a rumble,
And so dear old wife of mine,
I think we must prepare to dine.

It's nearly 4, the hour's late!
My dear we mustn't hesitate,
To get a light under the pan,
Please hurry – go quick as you can!

I'm weary and I'm fading fast.
So hungry I don't think I'll last.
It doesn't take that long to make,
It's nearly 5 for heaven's sake!

Dinner is served at 4.55.
It's a wonder that I'm still alive.
There really wasn't time to lose,
I nearly missed my PM snooze.

# BEIGE

Have you seen the youth of today?
You've seen the clothes they wear?
My word, those jazzy patterns
Would give anyone a scare!
And the colours! Oh the colours
- They are terribly bright!
I should walk around wearing sunshades
So I don't damage my sight.

I could show them a thing or two
A woman of my age.
The thing you must remember is
You can't go wrong with beige!

## Slow Lane

Drivers must go fast today,
And beep if you get in their way.
It's really not the way to go,
There's much more pleasure driving slow.
The road ahead is open, bare,
As I motor on without a care.
The world behind me loud and brash,
I wonder if there's been a crash?
As traffic's snarled up pretty bad,
Oh boy, oh boy I'm mighty glad,
That I am heading up the lane,
Not stuck back there, that looks a pain.

# Retirement

The day you have been waiting for
Has finally arrived.
Your working days are over
And you've made it out alive.
The world it is your oyster,
You can do just as you please.
Well, for as long as you stay mobile,
Please go careful on the knees.
And only in fine weather
- Rain and ice could cause a slip.
As at your grand old age that
Would surely break a hip.
But think of all the hobbies
You can do now that you're free.
The jigsaws and the book clubs,
And of course daytime TV.
They'll be more time with the grandkids,
Maybe more than you can bear.
Now that you're no longer working
You will be the child care.
And all day with your loved one -
How utterly sublime.
Now that you are home all day
They can nag you all the time.
Retirement has it's pro's and con's
But take it on the chin –
As long as you stay above the ground
Consider it a win!

# Queue

Since I retired,
There's nothing much to do.
I like to wander round and find
Myself a good old queue.
It doesn't matter where,
I care not of the venue.
But it gets me out the house
To stand and chat, when in a queue.

Sometimes I stand and grumble,
Or meet a friend anew.
Sometimes I just stay silent
And pass judgement on the few.
I really could quite happily spend
My whole day in a queue.
At least it gets me out
And gives me something to do.

# Manhood

There once was a time,
Not that long ago,
When my mighty manhood,
Could put on a great show.
Each and every morning,
Before I'd open my eyes,
He would always be
The first one of us to rise.
The cheeky wee fella,
And mischief he'd bring.
Every chance that he got,
From my trousers he'd spring.
Now his vigour has left him,
His light has gone out.
His remaining use,
Is that of water spout.
He lies in hibernation,
Behind all my zippers.
I need half a blue pill,
Not to piss in my slippers.
How it fills me with sadness,
To see him this way.
What a nighty beast he was,
Back in his heyday.

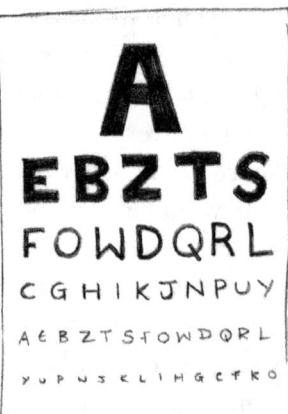
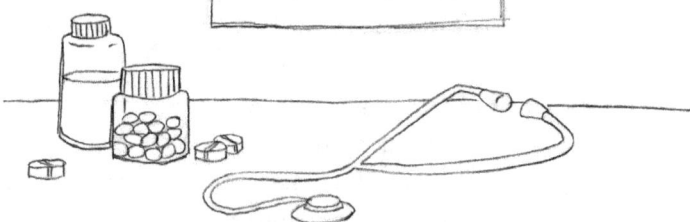

# The Doctor Will See You Now

Things are looking awfully bleak,
I'm at the doctors every week,
I give my blood, pee in a cup,
My dodgy back keeps playing up,
I have a gammy leg and hip,
They take in turns to give me jip,
My memory has got the shrinks,
My hearing absolutely stinks,
I need new spec's, I cannot see,
I'm having trouble when I pee,
I cannot breathe without a wheeze,
Don't even ask about the knees,
My blood pressure has gone sky high,
My cholesterol score will make you cry,
It seems old age has come to me,
It isn't what I thought it'd be.
If this is all there is alas,
The golden years can kiss my ass!

# EARLY

I like to rise with the sun.
I mustn't be late.
So many noisy tasks to complete,
That I mustn't hesitate.
The best part of the day,
Is before the world has risen.
And I'm thankful for this peaceful hour,
The gift I have been given.
For whilst the others are fast asleep,
Sweet dreams filling their heads.
I like to whip the mower out,
And shake them from their beds.
The perfect time for DIY?
6am I'm sure you'll agree.
Using a masonry drill at this hour,
Well, it makes me so happy.
You may say I'm a little cruel,
You may well think me mean.
But would you wish to deny me,
The one pleasure that I glean.
You have to take some fun in life,
Wherever you can.
And I'm afraid this is the thing,
That makes me a happy man.
So, I'll crash about in the garage,
And I'll bang around the house.

And once I have gotten you up,
I'll be as quiet as a mouse.
As all this early action,
Even though good for the soul.
Tires out a man of my age,
It really takes its toll.
So once they're up and off to work,
And I'm a happy chap.
I'll snuggle in my armchair,
And I'll take a little nap.

# I Am Not Old

I am not old. Not by a long way.
Mature maybe, but still in my heyday.
My eyes are just fine,
It's my arms that are wrong.
They print the words small now,
And my arms aren't that long.
I do not need a cane,
It's an implement of fashion.
I like to stay stylish,
It's always been a passion.
My hearing is perfect,
I just wish you wouldn't whisper.
And please do not mumble,
Pronounce your words crisper.
The lines on my face,
Are just crinkles from bed,
It's not grey but silver highlights,
That flow from my head.
I am not old. Not by a long way.
Mature maybe. But still in my heyday.

## Pill Poppin'

Hear me rattle, hear me shake,
With all the pills I have to take.
Such a sorry sight is me,
More tablets than the pharmacy.
I've some for back and some for knees,
There's some to help improve the wheeze,
I've some for heart, and some for blood,
Pill poppin' pensioner in the hood!
My stash all laid out in a tray,
That sorts out what I need each day.
Not just so that I feel alive,
But really so I can survive!
How I miss the days of yore,
And feeling how I felt before.
Old age creeps up and then is sprung,
Youth is wasted on the young.

# Forgetter

I'm not good at remembering
But my forgetter's getting strong.
I know your face, I know the place,
The name though has simply gone.

I will start to tell a story,
But will stop again part way.
I've forgot where I was headed,
I can't remember what to say.

I can walk into any room
And wonder why I'm there.
I came in with such purpose,
But should I really be elsewhere?

I will put things in a safe place,
You know this ends badly.
As the only problem with this is
It only makes them safe from me!

Yes, I'm not good at remembering
But my forgetter's getting strong.
Have we met before?
I know your face, but could be wrong.

# Father's Chair

Please come in and have a seat,
Please take the weight from off your feet,
But no, you mustn't sit just there,
That you see is father's chair.
It's just for him it's for no other,
He won't even let our mother.
Man of the house, it is his throne.
So it's for him, and him alone.
A status symbol some might say,
Or message to us to 'stay away'.
The chair arrived when did first child,
His piece of calm amidst the wild.
'Do not disturb' the message clear,
'You can be seen, don't let me hear
A peep from you whilst in my chair',
Not to be bothered when sat there,
A right of passage for all men,
Apart from the shed, this is their den.
No none of us would ever dare,
To go and sit in father's chair.

# MOT

I went to see the doctor,
For my annual MOT.
He poked and prodded, did his tests,
And then said, 'Dearie me'.
The seal is gone around the rear,
The gas is leaking fast.
The legs look quite unsteady,
I don't know if they can last.
Your hearing is abysmal,
And I'm surprised that you can see.
Many alarm is going off,
When I dip and test your pee.
'And the good news?' I ask hopefully,
Well he stopped to think this through.
Your teeth are all quite perfect,
But then those dentures are brand new!

## Computer Says No

I'm not a techy whizz kid.
I think it's fair to say.
The trouble is we didn't have
these things back in my day.
Computer-mi-bobs and the interweb,
Is there really any need?
Let's all slow down and take our time,
Do we really need such speed?
I prefer my text on paper,
Like my mail through the door,
My shopping done on the high street,
Checking the paper for the score.
For weather I have a window,
I do not need an app.
To talk to friends I'll call them up,
I don't need a screen to tap.
The world moves much too fast now.
Take a breath, go with the flow.
You'll find it far more pleasant,
When the computer says – 'no'.

## Older Than I Should Be

I'm older than I should be.
My mind's still in its youth.
It's just my poor old body,
That has got long in the tooth.
Inside I am still twenty-one,
I am a coiled spring.
My body will just laugh though,
'Ha! You must be joking!'

*I cannot hoist you from the floor,*
*No, you can't run anymore,*
*Please only walk if there's a seat,*
*There's far too much weight on your feet,*
*You cannot dance, you'll break a hip,*
*Without your glasses you'll see zip!*

I do try to ignore it.
I try to tell it 'shush!'.
I always start and have a go,
Give the body a push.
But it's a stubborn so and so.
I know it will always win.
So I snuggle with book and knitting bag,
Looks like I'm staying in.

## 50 Shades of Beige

She put down the remnants of her drink,
She turned to him and gave a wink,
Said 'I'm going up to bed my dear',
Then just to make sure he was clear,
She allowed her dressing gown to slip,
As she stood there posed with hand on hip.

Message received, he understood,
Though he was unsure if he could.
To conserve his strength and save the climb,
He took the stair lift up this time.
He found her lying on the bed.
His face blushed very slightly red.
He aimed to look both bold and mighty,
But couldn't work her winceyette nighty.
Confused and frustrated he just sat,
Then with a tut said 'bugger that!'
And in a small partial retreat,
He slipped himself beneath the sheet.

She leant across, gave him a kiss,
But without glasses she did miss,
And got him square in his left eye.
'ahh-yer bugger!' he let cry.
She lent again, he grabbed her ass.
She popped her false teeth in a glass,
And gave a gummy, toothless grin,

It sent a shiver 'cross his skin.
Patiently she lay there waiting,
What's with all the hesitating?
In truth though he could not begin,
Until the special pills kicked in.

To stall for time they kissed and cuddled,
But before long they both were muddled.
Which really was an awful shame,
As neither remembered their aim,
And so instead with confused frown,
They prepared for sleep and settled down.

She turned to him a little shy,
(Although she was quite unsure why)
'I love you my dear with all my heart'
He responded with a snore and fart.
And that's the tale of love grown old,
A truer love tale never told.

# My Way

I know what I like,
And I like what I know.
If I don't want to go there,
I'm not gonna go.
If I don't want to speak,
I will hang up the phone.
If I don't want to see you,
I'll pretend I'm not home.
If I don't want to go out,
Then I'll sit in my chair.
I'm too old to worry,
And I'm too old to care.
Take me as you find me.
I'll put on no show.
I know what I like,
And I like what I know.

# Of Age

I am of the age where I can lose my phone,
As I hold it in my hand.
Where I can forget where I was going,
By the time it takes to stand.
Where my joints take time to limber,
Protesting movement with a creak.
Where a laugh, a cough, or sneeze,
Will produce a little leak.
I can remember my whole childhood,
But yesterday? Not a clue.
I will call out every name I know,
Before I get to you.
Where the day is not complete unless,
I've had a nap or two.
Where I barely lift a finger yet,
I'm gasping for a brew.
Where I'm losing my hair from my head,
And sprouting places new.
Oh this getting old malarkey
Is a right hullabaloo!

# Age Test

There is an easy age test,
Of which I have been told.
It really is quite simple,
And will determine if you're old.

Step one is find a busy street,
We need people around.
Step two (here comes the fun part),
Throw yourself upon the ground.

The result's in the reaction,
What onlookers do after.
If you're still young, the crowd around
Will all erupt in laughter.

If though you are deemed as old,
As on the ground you're laid.
You will hear their gasps of panic,
As they rush to give you aid!

# Lost

I thought I could find it
But it's gone without trace.
It isn't lost
Just in a safe place.
My things keep on moving
A trick being played.
I go to where it should be
But it seems to have strayed.
My glasses for instance,
Required quite the rummage.
Not sat in their case
But instead sat in the fridge!
The newspaper in the greenhouse,
My keys in the cake tin.
I don't understand it,
My head's in such a spin.
I only found my phone
when it started to ring
and I have to say
it's most disconcerting.
Am I going senile?
Can it really be me?
More likely a prankster
I'm sure you'll agree.

# I Am Old

I am old. Or so I've been told.
Well I hate to argue,
But my hips are brand new.
And these teeth that you see?
2003.
So less of the old,
I scold.

I am an old fart.
Well that cuts to the heart.
So let me tell you straight,
I am still up to date.
I am hip and on trend,
Do you comprehend.
I just hide it well,
So nobody can tell,
A secret power for me,
To see.

## Grumbles

At this age of mine
Though things are all fine
Listen close, I'll speak clear, I won't mumble.
You'll find life does improve
From the moment you choose
To let loose and let rip a good grumble.

Even when life is bliss
Just look closely, don't miss
All the niggles and wrongs that pass by.
From the state of your shoes
To the weather and news
Put them straight and let your grumbles fly!

# Pipe and Slippers

Retiree's life can be awfully tough,
Us OAPs we have it rough,
The early hour we start our day,
The tiredness that won't go away,
Visits and playtime with the nippers,
Is rectified, with pipe and slippers.

Everything takes longer to complete,
My favourite foods, I now can't eat,
Cholesterol has laid end to that,
Everything has too much salt or fat,
Big movements will leave me achy,
But all is better, with a cup of tea.

I pee more than I am asleep,
My bald spots bigger than my sweep,
Change is feared, and new is scary,
My nose and ears are awfully hairy,
The slightest knock will leave a bruise,
But all is well, reading the news.

# I am Grandad

I am Grandad, come and play,
I'll show you how it's done my way.
We may get muddy, may get wet,
But we'll have fun, so don't you fret.
We'll dig the garden, race the snails,
With grass stained knees and dirty nails.
We'll wash the car and play some ball,
A fireman's lift if you should fall.
We'll climb the trees and look for nests,
Be told off when we tear our vests.
We'll get the toolbox, we'll saw and screw,
And make ourselves something brand new.
We'll sit down when our work is done,
And look back over all our fun.
You'll snuggle close and find a nook,
And together we will share a book.

## Good for What Ails You

If you eat your crusts, I swear,
It will give you luscious curly hair.
A coin in boiled egg (no lie),
Will get rid of a blackened eye.
Spinach on your ear you need,
To help when you have a nosebleed.
In your sock an onion or two,
To cure you of the cold or flu.
Bread and milk paste (don't recoil),
Spread upon a nasty boil.
This one's much nicer so do take note,
Take marshmallows to soothe a sore throat.
When I have Grandma's home remedy,
I do not need a pharmacy.
Although sometimes there's no way to tell,
If the cure will work or just make you smell!

## Old Fart

He is just an old fart
Pulling on a shopping cart
Making people wait a while
As he blocks the shopping aisle
He doesn't see, he's unaware
Or maybe he just doesn't care
The people tut, he's in their way
But he won't rush, he's got all day
And so he'll potter, take his time
I doubt he even hears them whine
They're far too busy for their own good
They should slow down, if only they could
But there's places that they need to be
So they send out a silent plea
For him to move, pick up the pace
But he knows that it's not a race
He's quite content, he doesn't worry
As those around him try to hurry
So please watch out on aisle eight
If you go down, you will be late
There is a blockage with a cart
As we all wait for the old fart

# I Am Granny

I am Granny, come and stay,
We have so much that we can play.
I have a recipe we can bake,
Together we can make a cake,
And ice it blue with chocolate drops,
Better than you'd find in the shops.

Grab your paper, crayons too,
And we'll draw pictures of the zoo,
The circus, fair or treasure maps,
With pirate booty and their traps,
We'll lay a board out as a prank,
And then make Grandad walk the plank.

We'll paint, do puzzles, read and sew,
We'll snuggle up and watch a show,
Then pour some tea out in the break,
And then return with some of our cake.

# Back In My Day

Kids today have life so easy,
Well sit down while I tell a story to thee.
Back in my day, didn't you know,
We had to walk twenty miles through snow.
This was everyday as a rule.
Just so that we could go to school,
And it was uphill both ways.
That's just what you did back in them days.

You could go to the cinema with a penny,
Not just get the one film but many.
The movie, a cartoon and the news,
Some popcorn and some fruity chews,
And if that wasn't enough for thee,
You'd still have change for a chippy tea.

Kids today are spoilt rotten,
Look at all the tat they've gotten.
So many toys it makes you sick,
We only had one – and that was a stick.
We never complained though, that was enough.
Back in my day, life was tough.

## Bus Pass

I never drove it very far
So I decided I would sell the car
I'm retired so bus pass for me
I shall travel everywhere for free
It's true the journey takes much longer
And the smell of urine's definitely stronger
And sometimes they can be late
But that's no reason you should hate
The bus can be a pleasant place
And A to B is not a race
Besides they leave quite frequently
And with my pass I travel free

# CHANGE

I like things just the way they are,
Why do they have to change?
If things are working well,
Then there's no need to rearrange.
With everything I use it seems,
It has become my fate,
That as soon as I conquer it,
It gets a new update!

Well this trend has to stop,
I think that we should take a stand.
It's surely just a marketing ploy,
And so it should be banned.

I do not need a new phone,
I can make calls with this with ease.
Do not mess with my computer,
I beg of you now please.
The TV's set how I like it,
If you alter it just know,
That I will hunt you down,
If you make me miss my show.

## Looks Good to Me

Looking in the mirror
I look mighty fine
Not a single wrinkle
Not a single line
My house is spotless
Just look around
Not a cobweb or speck of dust to be found
The garden is tidy
The grass looks grand
Everything looks so much better than planned
So much so
that I'm not sure when
I shall ever wear my glasses again!

## Volume Control

I think the TV's broken,
Everyone is so soft spoken.
It never used to be this way,
I turn the volume up each day.
It used to sit quite nice at 10,
But then time and time again,
I'd find I'd struggle to make out,
What everyone was on about,
And so, before we knew,
We had it turned up to 32.

## Charm & Grace

Us ladies of advancing years
Who are now safe from the builder's jeers
We may drink a little too much gin
And have the odd whisker on our chin
We have gone soft around the middle
A laugh's been known to induce some piddle
Our bra-less boobs will graze our thigh
We'll wear our knickers nice and high
With anti-wrinkle cream on our face
We will age with charm and grace
Or at least we'll give it a good try
There's still a sparkle in our eye

## How Old?

As children we're proud of our age,
We show it off with glee.
Our enthusiasm for this
Starts to fade from age twenty.
We will hide it or deny it,
We'll count back and we will lie.
From twenty-five to retirement
On our age we do go shy.
But from sixty comes freedom
And once again we are proud.
We don't care who knows it
We'll tell all and tell them loud.
The sign that you are really old
Comes with the next reaction.
When asked you break it down some more
By adding on the fraction.
Not ninety but ninety and a half
You answer bursting with pride.
With childlike excitement
Twinkling eyes and smile wide.

# I'd Rather Dye

My hair is turning silver
I hide it all from show
I cover it with hair dye
So that no one can know
It started with a stray one
That snuck in unannounced
It hung there bright and shiny
Its presence to be flounced
I attacked it with the tweezers
I showed it who was boss
But it seems the little bugger
Just didn't give a toss
He came back a few weeks later
This time he brought some friends
Plucking wasn't the answer
I saw where this one ends
So I marched down to the salon
Yes, I was prepared to buy
My way back into victory
Every strand had to dye!

# Key to Success

Success when aged 4 is keeping your pants dry
Getting to the toilet on time
If you fail don't deny

Success when aged 8 is finding your own way home
On the first try if possible
Without having to roam

Success when aged 12 is having good friends
Your whole social standing
On this depends

Success when aged 17 is driving a car
Without that licence
You'll not get very far

Success when aged 20 is having sex
With an actual person
Not just the Kleenex

Success at 35 is having money
It certainly makes life
So much more sunny

Success when aged 60 is still having sex
At least there's no longer need
For the Durex

Success at 65 is still driving a car
You may still have your licence
But can you go far?

Success when aged 70 is finding your own way home
On the first try if possible
Without having to roam

Success when aged 80 is keeping your pants dry
Getting to the toilet on time
If you fail don't deny

# To Pee or Not to Pee

Oh me oh my, oh my oh me,
Why do I so often have to pee?
It would appear my bladder's shrunk.
It cannot hold all that I've drunk.
If I pass a loo (you never know),
I'll go in case I have to go.
It's always worth a try you see,
And every time I'll do a wee.
My bladder barely holds a cup,
Before I'm totally filled up.
I cannot sleep the whole night through,
Without several journeys to the loo.
I really have quite come to hate,
This frequent need to urinate.
At least it keeps me on my feet,
Not vegging in my seat.

## Dinner time

Meat and two veg is the order of the day,
I know what I like, and I like it my way.

The mash must be creamy,
The meat cooked right through.
It shouldn't melt in the mouth,
You are supposed to chew.
If it's red then it's raw,
Please remove from my plate.
I know what I like, and I know what I hate.

Please keep my food plain,
I won't tolerate spice.
You may call it plain,
But I call it nice.
Pasta and rice, I will most likely snub.
I like good hearty food,
Proper English grub.
And yes, when without,
I've been heard to mutter,
That it is not a meal,
Without side bread and butter.

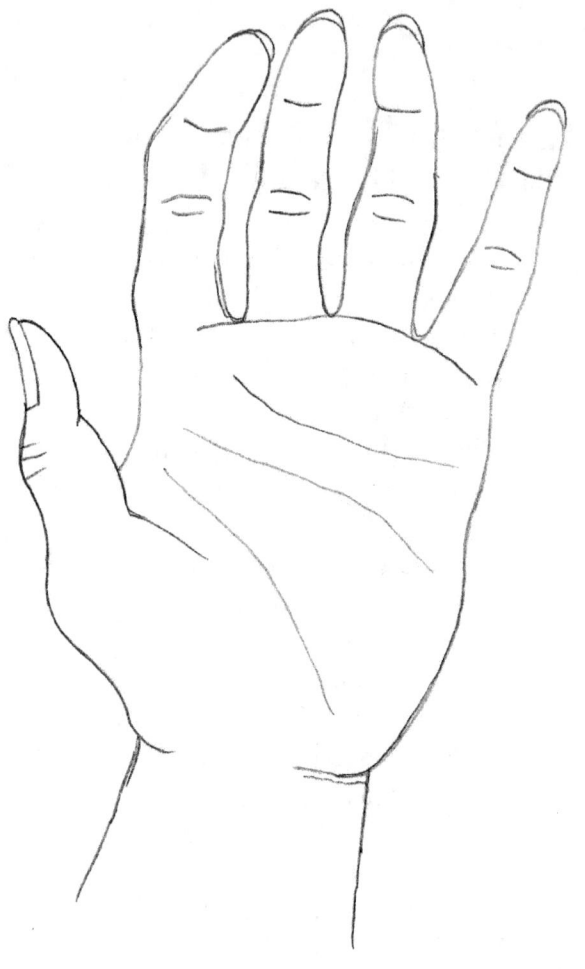

# My Hands

Who do these hands belong to?
These hands are not my own.
These hands are old and wizened,
Just skin and knobbly bone.

My hands are soft and delicate,
My hands have raised a child.
These nails are weak and discoloured,
My nails are always styled.

The joints in these are painful,
They don't work as they should.
Movement no longer easy,
They don't do what once they could.

I'm saddened by their aging,
I feel I've lost a tool.
They make me slow and clumsy,
They make me feel a fool.

Who do these hands belong to?
These hands are not my own.
These hands are old and wizened,
Just skin and knobbly bone.

# Revenge

I love my grandkids dearly,
I dote on them all day,
And so I really love it,
When the darlings come to stay.

But there's a secret behind it,
I use it as pay back.
A revenge on my children,
For all the times they gave me flack.

I get the grandkids all excited,
I fill them full of sweets.
I make sure they have non-stop fun,
I send them home with 'treats'.

They leave here crazed and hyper,
They're bouncing off the wall.
They'll be long gone and back at home,
Before they crash and fall.

Sweet revenge for all the backchat,
For all the sleepless nights,
The tears and all the tantrums,
For every pointless fight.

It's your turn now my children,
Have fun enjoy the ride.
"They weren't like this before you got here"
I say, while smile I try to hide.

They're unconvinced but say goodbyes,
With quick kiss and embrace.
And then I wave them off,
With innocent look upon my face.

## Life Happens When You're Busy

Life happens when you're busy,
Passes by, in the blink of an eye,
Flown by before you know,
Leaves you wondering; where did it go?

Life happens when you're not watching,
What was ahead, behind you has fled,
Dreams turned to memories to hold,
More precious to you than gold.

Life still has so much to give,
So enjoy every moment you live,
Take it with both hands in strong hold,
You story is still being told.

# Poor Old Pensioners

Poor old pensioners are we,
With tartan blankets on our knee,
Cataracts so thick we cannot see,
Oh woe, oh woe is me.

We can do just as we please,
Although it can't be done with ease,
And it will probably make us wheeze,
Or else be murder on the knees.

So please I think you ought,
To spare us old folk some thought,
For poor old pensioners are we,
Oh woe, oh woe is me.

## Always Read the Label

Please always read the label,
You must not ever guess.
Otherwise I guarantee,
You'll end up in a mess.
I found this out quite recently,
T'was just a week ago.
I went to get some pain meds,
After bashing my big toe.
The pills were in the bathroom,
But my specs were down the stair.
I thought it too much effort,
To go all the way down there.
God knows what I got hold of,
But it didn't go too well.
My heart started to race,
And certain parts began to swell.
'Whey hey' I thought it's not all bad,
I'll go and find my lass.
It wasn't till I burst in,
I remembered her book class.
Ten blue rinse beauties,
Were staring back at me.
One feinted, several blushed,
And poor old Mildred spilt her tea.

My wife, aghast, was furious.
I thought quickly of what to say.
'Oh is it not life drawing'
'I must have the wrong day'.
To spare my blushes I reached out,
To grab and cover with a hat.
But in all of the kerfuffle,
I only went and grabbed the cat.
Long story short I'm healing well,
The wife's back talking to me.
Recounting the story,
Was not believed by A&E.
The book club has recovered,
Though some still remain unsure,
And so future meets,
Can't be at our house anymore.

# Doolally

Will you still visit when I'm senile?
Will you see me when I'm dotty?
Will you help me find my marbles,
When I've gone a little potty?
When I'm mad as a hatter,
Will you still come to tea?
Imagine all the fun we'll have,
When I've gone doolally.

# With Thanks

A huge thank you to everyone who
knowingly or not contributed to this book.
It has been a very amusing journey
and I hope you enjoy the results.

Thank you to my two editors and proof readers
the wonderful Gary Parker and Carol Page.

# Others in the series....

There are also many other books by Gemma
check out her website:

## WWW.GEMMADENHAM.COM

for more information, or follow her
@gemmaEdenham  gemmadenhamauthorillustrator

www.ingramcontent.com/pod-product-compliance
Lightning Source LLC
Chambersburg PA
CBHW071737080526
44588CB00013B/2063